The Word of the Christ of God
to Mankind, Before this World Passes Away

Nearer to God in You

GU00985334

The Word
of the CHRIST OF GOD
to Mankind,
Before this World Passes Away

Nearer to God in You

THE WORD
THE UNIVERSAL SPIRIT

First Edition 2007

Published by:
© Universal Life
The Inner Religion
P. O. Box 3549
Woodbridge, CT 06525
U S A

Licensed edition
translated from the original German title:
"Das Wort des CHRISTUS GOTTES an die
Menschheit, bevor diese Welt vergeht.
Näher zu Gott in dir."

From the Universal Life Series
with the consent of
© Verlag DAS WORT GmbH
im Universellen Leben
Max-Braun-Strasse 2
97828 Marktheidenfeld/Altfeld
Germany

Order No. S 139 en

The German edition is the work of reference for all
questions regarding the meaning of the contents.

ISBN 978-1-890841-45-4

Table of Contents

Introduction

The word of God at this time is the greatest gift of heaven to mankind. Directly in the prophetic word and through Gabriele, His prophetess and spiritual ambassador, God, the Eternal, tells us everything that is important for us human beings to know. He tells us what we need in order to understand the great spiritual correlations and to recognize everything that is taking place in the world in its background, in its enigmatic depths and in its deceitfulness. He also explains how every person can walk the path back into the eternal homeland through the true teachings of Jesus, the Christ, through the active application of the divine commandments and of the Sermon on the Mount of Jesus in daily life.

In August of 2005, the Christ of God gave us an encompassing revelation, which He Himself titled with the following words:

The Word of the Christ of God
to Mankind, Before this World Passes Away
Nearer to God in You

An Original Christian outlined its contents in the following way:

"In a mighty revelation, the Christ of God directed His word to mankind, before this world passes away. To show the caste of priests their cruel deeds, He held up a mirror, which today gives a similar picture as 2000 years ago:

The priests of today are descendants of descendants of descendants, who persecuted and still persecute the true prophets, who incited and still incite the people who had Jesus crucified, who twisted and still twist the word of God and who preached and still preach the doctrine of idolatry to the people. He raised the accusation that they steal from people and nations, piling up their wealth while looking on, unmoved, as whole nations die of hunger, illness and disease. He held up to them how hypocritically, as counterfeiters and idolaters, they raise themselves above the people in gold-embellished robes, abusing the one God for their cult of idols. He prophesied the end of the blind leaders of the blind and their subjects and lemmings, and announced the victory of truth.

Through a woman whom He made His prophetess, He, the Spirit of truth, gave the word of truth in this mighty turn of time, having taught and still teaching people about the near God.

After settling accounts with the descendants of descendants of descendants of the caste of priests and their dependents, the Spirit of the Christ of God again spoke of His simple and ingenious teaching – a summary, so to speak, of the Inner Path, which during our time in recent years, He has brought close to us in all detail. This summary of the Inner Path spans a great bow which is upheld by the divine rule of life: *Do not do to others what you do not want to have done to you.*

Whoever accepts and receives this summary of the Inner Path from our Redeemer, Jesus, the Christ, fulfilling it in his daily life, no longer needs the loud hullabaloo that leads people to without, covering His work and life as Jesus of Nazareth with rites, dogmas and ceremonies. His words lead us out of the dark enclosures of the churches and cathedrals, and toward the light that shines in the very basis of our soul, in the innermost recesses of every person."

In His revelation, Christ said that on this short Inner Path, He is "giving instructions for a higher life."

The word of the Lord, of the Christ of God, comes alive in the hearts, in the consciousness, of those who strive to follow Him. They know that the unending power and light of God is effective in His word for the people who accept and receive it. The divine energy flows to every willing person who strives to apply His instructions in his daily life, in his thinking, speaking and doing, thus letting them become fruitful.

A small group of Original Christians in Universal Life came together with Gabriele to talk with each other about the words of the Christ of God in His revelation. The content of this conversation is recorded in this small book, so that everyone who wants to can attain a higher life, a life in the Spirit of God, led and guided by Christ.

Faith

Following are the words of the Christ of God, from His great revelation of August 2005, on the topic "Nearer to God in You."

... As Jesus of Nazareth, I taught that the word of God should be done, that is, fulfilled. I essentially said: The one who hears My words and acts accordingly is like a wise man who built his house on the rock. When now a cloudburst came and the floods rose and the winds blew and beat upon that house, it did not collapse, because it had been built on rock. But everyone who hears My words and does not act accordingly is like a foolish man who built his house on sand. When now a cloudburst came and the floods rose, and the winds blew and beat against that house, it collapsed and was totally destroyed.

The caste of priests teaches that faith alone is enough. However, the soul of a human being is on earth to recognize the burdens it has inflicted upon itself, to repent of them and to clear them up. And if the person no longer commits the same mistakes, his soul fills with light. The path of the soul in a human being is: Learn, in order to become divine again. The path into the eternal Father-house begins with faith and the step-by-step fulfillment of the divine rule of life.

Faith alone, without the fulfillment of the commandments of God and the teachings that I, as Jesus of Nazareth, proclaimed is like a hollow fruit. This hollow faith is a blind faith that keeps those who cling to it blind, inviting them to continue to sin. This is agreeable to the caste of priests, because they, who lead the people astray, are the greatest sinners.

What is true faith?

True faith is the active faith, the step-by-step fulfillment of My teachings. If you, O human being, want to learn to believe, then keep the following rule of life, which leads you into the details of the commandments of God and into the essence of the Sermon on the Mount. The rule of life that includes the commandments of God and the Sermon on the Mount is the following: Do to others as you would have them do to you. Or said differently: Do not do to others what you do not want to have done to you.

As Jesus of Nazareth I taught the people who wanted to follow Me to go into a quiet chamber, which means to seek out a quiet place where the person is alone with *himself and with God, his eternal Father. This quiet place is now more necessary than ever, because this world has become ever louder, ever more hectic and brutal. Nature also offers stillness and reflection to a person who wants to turn within to the Spirit of the Christ of God, who I Am in the Father. In nature, away from the loud hustle and bustle and din of the human ego, to be alone with God, with His creation, the person striving toward God experiences the pulsating life, the Spirit of infinity.*

When you pray, O human being, be it in your quiet chamber or in nature, then remember My words: "Do to others as you would have them do to you." Or said differently: "Do not do to others what you do not want to have done to you." You will soon recognize that this all-encompassing divine law of inner life applies not only to people, but also to nature, to the animals, to everything that lives on, in and above the earth. If you remember this all-encompassing rule of life over and over again, your prayers will become more deeply heartfelt, because you are following the divine advice: nearer to God in you.

Very gradually, the desire to fulfill your prayers more and more in daily life will rise out of the depths of your being. If you follow this desire, you will experience the inner guidance to a fulfilled life.

In the modest contentment that the true, the inner, life brings with it, another desire will ripen very gradually. This, too, flows out of the depths of your awakened soul and, after you have prepared for the day, stimulates you to link with Me, the Spirit of love in you, in the very basis of your soul, so that you begin the day with Me, the Spirit of truth. If you also fulfill this desire of your soul, you will think ever more often during the day of the rule of life: "Do not do to others what you do not want to have done to you" – above all when difficulties with your fellowmen arise or when serious problems come up at work, for instance, when something is demanded of you that you reject because of personal ideas or ambitions and the like.

The day brings many hints to every person, often of a very painful kind. But every hint – be it an ever-so-great turning point in the day or even in your whole life – has a message or answer for the one concerned. If the emotions of the one concerned come into turmoil, then he cannot fathom right away what message this situation or that difficulty wants to convey. Later, when he has calmed down, perhaps in the evening, *those things the day reflected to him may then become apparent.*

To close the day becomes a necessity for the one who applies active faith and the rule of life, so that he may correctly sort through in his consciousness the disagreeable situations, but also what was agreeable. Through this, he can become calm again, which for every person is the key to the inner stillness that the Christ of God is in the very basis of each soul – the I Am, the Spirit, which speaks to the people through the prophetic word and is giving instructions in this text for a higher life. The place of stillness, which the one striving toward God has arranged in a room or in nature, becomes a necessity for the one who follows the desire of his soul, which has awakened in the awareness of the Eternal One. Particularly in the evening, when your work is done, when you linger in a quiet place in your earthly home, then light a candle, if you want to. The light of the candle symbolizes the inner light, the Spirit in your soul, to whom you are praying.

Why do I use the words of freedom – "if you want to" – over and over again? Know that the rule of life contains absolute freedom, which you also find in the commandments of God and in My teachings that I gave 2000 years ago as Jesus of Nazareth, and in My word today, the prophetic word. A human being is absolutely free to do or not do, as he prefers. From the mighty Creator, the human being received a conscience and a mind as a scale for weighing his thinking and doing. In addition, he also received the guidelines for weighing and measuring, the commandments of God and the divine wisdoms of life that I, the Christ of God, taught and still teach. These point out that the human being is himself responsible for what he does or does not do.

On your life's path to God, our eternal Father, you should know that no person can take away the "for and against" of another person. Nor can a pastor or priest take away from you what you have voluntarily inflicted upon yourself, for they are likewise sinners, and, as sinners, can forgive only those who have sinned against them.

Now I come back again to the closing of the day and to the prayer for the night.

You have gone into your quiet chamber, to a quiet place. Now let the day pass by you in review. It shows *you in pictures the events and situations of the day again. Remember the rule of life. Apply it, by comparing it to the events of the day. If it is difficult for you to apply the rule of life, which encompasses the commandments of God and My teachings of the Sermon on the Mount, then I advise you to take the commandments of God or the Sermon on the Mount in hand, depending on which you prefer. Read the divine laws calmly and reflectively, for they are given so that you can weigh and measure what the day reflected to you or even brought to you.*

How you decide is entirely up to you. If you want to master the events and situations of the day according to the rule of life, then go into prayer first. Ask for support and help. Soon you will experience that you are not alone, that I, the Spirit of the Christ of God, am active in you. What you have recognized that can be rectified, do now, that is, today, to the extent it is possible for you. Note down what can only be taken care of tomorrow or later and keep your notes at the place of prayer in your room, so that you see them when you approach it. They will remind you that you should put right what still needs to be cleared up.

Very soon, you will experience how helpful it is to close each day with My help. Then you will go into

17

the evening with the certainty that I Am with you. Before you go to sleep, thank the almighty, eternal Father for your life on earth, and make yourself aware that you are His son, His daughter, whom He loves, just as He loves all of His children, yes, His entire creation, all of infinity, including the nature kingdoms with their many kinds of animals and life forms. With this closing of the day, you place the night and your sleep in God's hands.

The next morning you will awaken and get up feeling fresher, more positive and joyful. Where was your soul while you were sleeping deeply? Do not try to explore this. If it has something to convey to you, the human being, you will know this in the morning. However, there is one thing that your alert soul striving toward God wants: that you, the person, begin the day with God.

If you do this as I have explained to you, and if you keep up your efforts to draw closer to God in you, you will also experience the Spirit of truth and love ever more often. The more you approach Me in the very basis of your soul, the greater are the steps that I will take toward you.

Know that every person who sets out to fulfill the rule of life will have to go through a "lean period," because the all-too-human debris, the wrongdoing, also called sins against the true life, must first be cleared away to such an extent that the light, which I Am, can reach the person more encompassingly, so that he may feel Me and gain the certainty that I Am the one who shines in him and through him, the Christ of God.

People also call this "lean period" the "night of the soul." If you do not despair and if you trust Me, then the day will spiritually dawn more and more in you. This becoming light-filled expresses itself in a transcendent quiet joy and thankfulness, which signals to you that you have taken several quite large hurdles. ...

Here follows the conversation
on the words of revelation of
Jesus, the Christ.

Let us become aware of what Jesus, the Christ, revealed through His prophetess: *The one who hears My words and acts accordingly is like a wise man who built his house on the rock. When now a cloudburst came and the floods rose and the winds blew and beat upon that house, it did not collapse, because it had been built on rock. But every one who hears My words and does not act accordingly is like a foolish man who built his house on sand. When now a cloudburst came and the floods rose, and the winds blew and beat against that house, it collapsed and was totally destroyed.*

In these words, Jesus, the Christ, the divine inspirer in today's time, spoke about acting according to His teaching, about doing, about the active faith. Thus, it becomes clear that "faith alone," as the church institutions teach, is of little use, because faith alone has no activity, and is therefore, a hollow faith.

Only the true doing helps us further on our path to the inner life, to a life that brings us peace, freedom, justice and inner happiness. *The one who hears My words and does them is like a wise man.* Or, as Christ expressed it in His revelation: *The one who hears My words and acts accordingly is like a wise man.*

So what can we do, to let our faith in God become active?

Belief is the prerequisite. For this reason, let us first ask ourselves: Do I believe in God? If we can affirm this, then the next question is: If I believe in God, what should I do to make this faith come alive?

The doing – as Christ also teaches us in His revelation – is the fulfillment of the divine rules of life, the daily striving to practice the divine laws in our day-to-day living. Consequently, it is not just about mere faith, but about fulfilling the commandments of God.

A particular concern of the Christ of God for us is the application of that commandment that He calls the "rule of life": *Do to others as you would have them do to you*. Or, said differently: *Do not do to others what you do not want to have done to you.*

The other one, the others – who are they? It is my neighbor, my fellowman, and in a broader sense, it is all the life forms of nature. If I want to draw closer to God, I cannot avoid examining my patterns of behavior toward my fellowmen and my fellow creatures, and changing them, wherever it is called for. Therefore, the first step that leads toward the fulfillment of this rule of life is the active faith.

This means that I first have to recognize that I am doing something to my neighbor that harms him, so that I can ask myself the question: "Do I want to be treated as I am treating my neighbor?" But this alone is not enough, because if I only say, "No, I don't," the active faith has not yet become an intrinsic part of myself.

The questions should be: "What do I want? How do I want to be treated? What do I have to do instead of my wrongdoing? What attitude do I now want to assume?"

Who will tell me what inner attitude I have to assume, so that I no longer commit my fault? – I find the answer in the commandments of God and in the teachings of Jesus, the Christ, primarily, in the Sermon on the Mount. And then, it is about changing what I have recognized accordingly. For Jesus, the Christ, revealed to us: *And if the person no longer commits the same mistakes, his soul fills with light.*

The Spirit of life said in His revelation: *The path of the soul in the human being is: Learn, in order to become divine again.* So, what should we learn, so that we find our way to our origin again, which is divine?

The basic questions are always: "Do I believe that I come from God? Do I believe that in God I am a free, happy being who can again take up the inner life, which is without sin, without wrongdoing?"

The Ten Commandments of God and the Sermon on the Mount of Jesus, the Christ, are the criteria that correspond to divine justice. This freedom, this happiness, which we again strive toward as intrinsically divine beings, should apply to all beings. And this path is open to all beings, if we human beings meet one another according to the justice of God.

What does justice mean, for example, to the youth?

For young people, justice means to basically apply the Golden Rule from the Sermon on the Mount: *Do to others as you would have them do to you.* That is to say: *Do not do to others what you do not want to have done to you.* In this, justice is manifest. And this justice would lead to the fact that things would go well for the people on earth, and not only for them, but also for the animal world, and all of nature. A young person still has an eye for the whole earth and can see the injustice of many things taking place in the world. Many people are poor, many are starving. All this could be changed if every single one would begin by fulfilling bit by bit the Golden Rule in his own life.

So a young person could say: "Well, but I don't do anything to my friends. I don't have anything against this or that person. I may not like him so much. I may turn my back on him, but I don't do anything bad to him." – And yet, why do I turn my back on him? What thoughts do I have about him? Isn't this also very decisive – particularly for young people?

It is more important than many a person in his youth may think, because it is during our young years that these thoughts are developed and built up. It practically begins in the schoolroom, or at the beginning of our professional training, where we reject certain people, not wanting to have anything to do with them, and thus, avoid them. If a person doesn't question himself on this pattern of behavior, if he doesn't think about himself – "Why do I actually do this? What is it specifically about this person that I don't like? Maybe I have the same thing in me" – then, this disparagement and exclusion of others gets worse and worse with age. In the end, I don't even notice any more that I am rejecting people or passing sentence on them. I am not aware of it anymore as a "wrongdoing," instead, I think it is "totally normal."

As I grow older, the whole thing turns into envy. I am envious of this or that about my neighbor. And "envy" is only a generic term. This generic term, "envy," contains many, many negative thoughts. Envy leads to a falling out, to quarrel and hatred. This shows that at an older age the contents of a person's world of thoughts have become ingrained. It is good to know about this, because then we can avoid such developments in time.

But let us return to faith. If I believe in the existence of God, then I should ask myself: Do I affirm a hollow faith, the faith that the church institutions teach, or do I move in active faith? If the latter is the case, then it would be necessary to question my thoughts, to examine what contents they have, because often our lips say something different than what lies behind the words, for example, negative thoughts or feelings. So I should honestly question what I think or what I say, including how I behave, that is, I should question whatever I am doing.

If we question everything that we express in our life, we will very quickly realize that if we only believe in God but think, speak and act as we have until now, then our faith is that of the institutional churches; it is a hollow faith. But it is different if I question myself and say: "I believe in God. Why did He give us the commandments? And why did Jesus give us His teachings – above all, the previously mentioned rule of life that contains everything in it?" This "why" may help us find our way out of a muddled, blind faith and into the light that Jesus, the Christ, announced to us in the words: *The one who hears My words and acts accordingly is like a wise man.*

And His words: *This hollow faith is a blind faith that keeps those who cling to it blind, inviting them to continue to sin* acquire additional meaning. The one who merely says "faith alone is enough" also doesn't try to eliminate his faults and sins, but will keep accumulating new ones.

While many an older person who already has his property and goods more or less in his back pocket, so to speak, very often simply accepts occurrences as they appear, the youth tend to be alert and critical and look at the world with different eyes. They also ask questions, perhaps among others, the following: "Who can prove to me that the institutional church belief, the so-called hollow faith, is not the right one?" In their eyes, it could look like this:

Particularly a look into the world shows that this blind faith does not bring about anything positive and for this reason cannot be the right one. For what has been achieved on this earth in the name of Jesus, the Christ, during the past 2000 years? And with this, has mankind drawn even one step closer to what Jesus announced at the end of His time on earth? Even then, wasn't His goal to establish the Kingdom of Peace? Conditions in the world today show quite clearly that it is worse than ever before. Let us look into nature, let us see how people live – nothing has improved through institutional faith during the 2000 years since Jesus of Nazareth; instead it has worsened many times over. This clearly shows that the institutional faith of the churches cannot be the true faith; otherwise, something would have changed toward the positive. Another indication is the fact that the fundamental questions of mankind have remained unanswered by the institutional faith. The vast majority of people are still asking in vain: "Where do I come from? Where am I going? What is the meaning of my life?" No pastor, no priest can give them conclusive, let alone satisfactory, information, or even an answer that would give them a hint where to look further.

Jesus, the Christ, said in His word for us today, *True faith is the active faith, the step-by-step fulfillment of My teachings,* that is, the teaching of God. And don't we know the saying, "You will recognize them by their deeds"? If we were to take a close look to where the caste of priests has led and is still leading those submissively dependent on them, we would be able to see what sort of people they are.

"You will recognize them by their deeds." The deeds of the caste of priests can be deduced from the state of today's world. Where has the caste of priests led its faithful, the faithful of the church?

It has led them into war, need, hunger, misery, illness, all those things that are hitting the people on the earth. The people could have used their minds, their thinking capacity, and avoided the manipulation in time. But the animals and Mother Earth were exposed to the arbitrary use of power by human beings. The adherents of the church institutions have become brutes toward nature and the animals, because the church princes, through their own way of life, set such an example for them, considering it right.

Many scientists today recognize that this world can no longer be saved. And where does the cause lie? Nature does not let itself be maltreated anymore by human beings. The severe natural disasters, the climatic changes, the earthquakes, the storms, all of these are an effect, a consequence, of what human beings have done to Mother Earth.

The people of western countries are so proud of the fact that the so-called Christian western world has had such definitive impact on the life of this earth. What does this impact look like? The allegedly Christian western world paid homage to the cult of idolatry of the priests and violated in barbaric ways the animals, the plants, the Mother Earth. This has now come to an end. The earth is rebelling. Whoever watches the correlations of events and analyzes them can only come to one conclusion: The greatest offense of that pagan cult lies in the fact that it prevented and did not teach the unity of man, nature and the animals, even though Jesus, the Christ, had taught and lived peace, love and the unity of all living things as an example for the people, over 2000 years ago.

That people are supposed to attend the so-called Holy Mass – as it is called by the priesthood – at least once a week also hasn't brought any gain. Week after week, many, very many people have attended various denominational worship services. But looking back, we ask: What have the worship services and the many prayers of the church faithful accomplished?

It has made the churches richer and the people poorer and, as already mentioned, it has brought out a complete disdain for all life. Human beings have not begun to take responsibility for themselves and to give an accounting of their lives before the laws of God.

And why? Because in the final analysis, in the institutional churches they say that "faith alone is enough." But it isn't enough! The proof lies before us. All the prayers in the churches, all the many, many worship services over the centuries – did any of it make the world a better place? There are countless "saints" in the Catholic Church. Many church faithful pray to the saints. What have the saints accomplished? Are people healthier? Is Mother Earth healthy? Are human beings peaceful? Again we ask the question: What did the many worship services and the many prayers of the church faithful accomplish? Very little or nothing at all, measured by the escalation of the "un-goodness" of our world today. However, 2000 years ago, Jesus, the Christ, taught us something completely different. He founded neither church institutions nor cathedrals.

What He said back then, He has again revealed during these days and over the last 30 years. Via the prophetic word, He said the following: *As Jesus of Nazareth I taught the people who wanted to follow Me to go into a quiet chamber, which means to seek out a quiet place where the person is alone with himself and with God, his eternal Father. This quiet place is now more necessary than ever, because this world has become ever louder, ever more hectic and brutal. Nature also offers stillness and reflection to a person who wants to turn within to the Spirit of the Christ of God, who I Am in the Father. In nature, away from the loud hustle and bustle and din of the human ego, to be alone with God, with His creation, the person striving toward God experiences the pulsating life, the Spirit of infinity.*

And Jesus, the Christ, continued to teach us via revelation on the short path to the higher life:

When you pray, O human being, be it in your quiet chamber or in nature, then remember My words: "Do to others as you would have them do to you." Or said differently: "Do not do to others what you do not want to have done to you."

Particularly in today's time – since the hustle and bustle, the noise, the loud and shrill dissonances lead so many, especially the young people, to believe that all of this is "life" and the intense enjoyment of life, and that these are important to them – does the advice of Jesus, the Christ, to go into a small, quiet chamber or to seek out nature, have any relevance at all?

At first glance, one would not think so.

Young people often long for those noises that in the world are equated with "life." They feel an urge to move forward; they want to achieve something; they want to experience what the world offers them. And it is completely normal for a young person to have such needs. There is nothing against experiencing it within certain parameters. But often, appearances deceive, because in a young person there is also just as much longing for the stillness. He notices pretty quickly that striving for the world and for what is found there isn't everything; instead, a longing rises from the depths of his inner being for something higher, for the good. If a young person hears this dynamic and simple teaching that the Christ of God Himself has given, then not seldom, he sits up and takes notice, thinking: "So, there is also this. It would be an alternative to try out."

Apropos withdrawing into the stillness – there are two possibilities for this. Unfortunately, one way often used by the youth is to escape into a dreamworld. This leads to unreality and not to living. The other way would be to do what Jesus, the Christ showed us, that is, to withdraw into the stillness and think about his own behavior and to become aware of the existence of God, of His presence.

This latter can be achieved by a young person particularly well in nature. If we open ourselves for the life, the expressions of life in the woods, on the fields and meadows, if we experience a flower that radiates something to us, if we perceive the sounds that nature brings out – whether it is the murmuring of the wind, the twittering of the birds or the fine chirping of a cricket – then we notice that on the earth there truly is something different than what the world offers. It makes a person feel peaceful, friendly; he feels a vastness that gives him confidence.

What does GOD mean to young people?

Certainly we cannot answer this question in the same way for all young people. For many of them, for example, those who have become acquainted with the fascinating and true teaching of Jesus, the Christ, God is, above all things, the kind, loving Father who loves each of His children equally, and we can turn to Him at any time. He supports each one in all the situations of the day; He always has an open ear for them; He is there for them at any time and always affirms the positive in each one, if the person himself resolves for it as well. And one or the other comes to realize that every now and then in his daily life the recognition flashes that "He is really there! And He guides everything to the good, if only we give Him the chance to do it!"

And what does God mean to an older person? Often, we experience that the name of God is sometimes filled with fear for an older person. But why fear of God? People on their way to God often experience that God is a loving Father. So why then, are so many people afraid of God?

Particularly in old age many things come up in us that we had previously repressed. It could be that our conscience, which we often pushed into the background, keeps breaking through and that many older people – if they make an accounting of their life – notice that they have done many things during their life that are not in accord with the divine laws as we know them from the Sermon on the Mount and the Ten Commandments. If this recognition keeps dawning in a person, what develops is a latent awareness of an insecurity, that is, a fear, because the person knows or feels that he was and is himself responsible for his life and that at some point, he can be called to account over a certain principle of the law.

It is possible that the following thought comes up in many people: "Now I am 50, 60, 70 or even more years old. Have I used my life on earth" – we speak of our earthly existence as our "life" – "at all well?"

In his conscious mind, many a one may nevertheless come to the conclusion that he never did anything to anyone and that he always tried to be a good person. But if it actually were so, then he should be free of fear – and despite this, the fear is there. And so, secretly, many people are actually aware of the fact that they did not make sufficient use of their earthly existence. They have an inkling of this and sense that just as they were and are as a human being, they do not want to meet up with God; they do not want to have to face Him.

Where does this inkling come from? In the end, it comes from the soul, which wants to once more give the older person a jolt and call to mind: *Do not do to others what you do not want to have done to you.*

If we put ourselves in the place of older people or the elderly, we notice an uneasy feeling that spreads out and weighs heavily in the stomach area because something isn't quite right with us. Perhaps pictures come up from the past that show us what we have done to others. Jesus spoke in the following sense: As long as you are still on your way with the "other," clear things up with him. So what applies here is to recognize – above all this includes older people – what is in conflict with the rule of life now or from your past, to feel remorse for it, to clear it up and do better from now on, by orienting yourself to the commandments of God and to the teachings of Jesus, the Christ.

37

Let it be said to young people: Today is the day of the Lord! Not in 10 or even 20 years. Today! And even if a young person is sometimes turned to without and may want to conquer the world from this or that point of view, if he dances and jubilates and is loud – please, this is a part of being young! But if behind everything that he does there is an awareness of the rule of life, *Do not do to others what you do not want to have done to you,* then in certain situations, he will suddenly have the feeling: "Wait a minute, I'm not going that far," namely, when he is on the verge of doing something that could harm the other, or nature, or the animal world.

Whoever builds into his human "computer world" the rule of life of Jesus, the Christ – *Do not do to others what you do not want to have done to you* – and keeps to it, will soon recognize that this all-encompassing lawful principle of inner life – for it does lead to the inner life! – not only applies to people, but also to nature and the animals and everything that lives on, in and over the earth. This generates the feeling of unity, a quality of life that makes a person free. And then, he will very soon feel what it means to have a fulfilled life.

What does a "fulfilled life" mean to a young person? This short Inner Path, which Christ has introduced to all people as a help for them, makes a person free and happy.

It is truly – in very plain words, very simple and easy to follow – the Inner Path, in summarized form. It is a great chance for many who want to take the hand of Christ and make use of their remaining days on earth. They will surely one day be very glad that they did not let this opportunity pass them by. And their soul also rejoices!

This short Inner Path, as we have now to some extent described it, makes a person above all self-reliant and independent of others. For by applying the Golden Rule of life – *Do not do to others what you do not want to have done to you* – each one of us finds his way to freedom. We no longer expect anything from our fellowman, that he does this or that for us. But then, we do not have to bind ourselves to our fellowman either, by fulfilling, in turn, his expectations. Why did we do this so often until now? Because ultimately, he fulfilled our expectations and desires.

Once again, especially for the young people: If the rule of life is "in the back of your mind" and it calls to you "Wait a minute, not like that," then you should also pause. Let's take a couple of examples of where this would be indicated:

When we, for example, exploit our neighbor, using him for something that could not only harm ourselves but him, as well.

When we say something unkind to our neighbor that he now struggles with. We should not do this, because, in the end, we also don't want someone to say something downright rude to us, even if it is the truth.

When we more or less force our neighbor to fulfill our sexual desires, without mincing words.

When we try to influence the other, thus detracting from his free will, that is, when we manipulate him. We may possibly be steering him in a direction that could be unfortunate for his future path through life. It could even go so far as to turn him completely away from his life's path.

Back to a question that hasn't been totally answered: Can it be that older people, who, for example, are afraid of God or are afraid of the future, are carrying their past as an engraving in their soul, which is calling out to them: "Clear up what happened in your youth now, in your middle age, or perhaps even in your old age?"

In the divine revelation Christ said: *The day brings many hints to every person, often of a very painful kind.* Such hints often nudge debts that are recorded in the soul of an older person. The person, who does not try to figure out in time what things are still latent in him, may be overcome with the fear we mentioned earlier.

With older people it is often so that they get upset over young people because they don't do things as the older people would like them to, or because they don't behave as the older person thinks they should. All these indicate that in the past we ourselves acted in the same way that we are now disapproving in others. Perhaps through the words of the Lord in His revelation, something has been brought into movement in this or that older person, so that he can now still use the opportunity to recognize what he did to others through his behavior in the past.

If many an older person wants to influence a younger person so that his own pattern is ingrained in the latter, isn't it envy that often lies behind this? Envy because the older person perhaps did not have or could not afford or did not dare to do in his own youth what this young person takes for granted, what this young person has, or how he can or is allowed to simply be?

Something like this must be behind such behavior. A self-possessed older person would never try to influence younger people, because he knows from his own experience that every person follows his own path. He will offer help, or support, insofar as the younger person obviously wants it, but he will never give instructions or try to pressure the other.

But such self-possession becomes an inherent part of an older person only when he has cleared up his past to a large extent.

Particularly in old age, we should think about being modest in our wants as Jesus, the Christ, talked about in His revelation. He revealed the following: *In the modest contentment that the true, the inner, life brings with it, another desire will ripen very gradually…* – and this desire could come from the awakened soul: that after getting ready for the day, the person pray to the Spirit of life which is found in the origin of his soul, thus beginning the day with Him.

To be modest in our wants applies to older people as well as to younger people. What do we understand by this modest contentment that Christ talked about?

Could it mean that we should begin to seek happiness in ourselves? After all, God dwells in us. That we should no longer expect happiness to be brought to us from without, or that others should make us happy. Instead, we should develop in ourselves the security in God, the relationship to God, the love for God. For to have communication with God, with Christ, in us is happiness – although it is a quiet happiness, a quiet joy, the feeling of being carried and supported by the stream of love and of the light of God.

We can understand that young people press forward, that they still have so many worldly desires. And it is important to fulfill many of your desires and wishes, but not lose sight of the Golden Rule of life while doing so. Wish for something that you can afford, but do not force your neighbor to fulfill your wishes, your desires.

As for older people, why are so many of them not modest in their wants? Modest contentment in an older person brings a certain freedom, a gratefulness, a self-possession, that bears in itself a higher image of the future.

This modest contentment is often not present because the past wasn't worked off. Perhaps we have the material possibilities to afford ever more luxuries, perhaps even to build a castle at an advanced age and spend a lot of money, because we believe that happiness lies in external things, having repressed our inner being, the knocking of our soul. But for many, such material possibilities don't exist. For them, this urge to show off, to affirm oneself, is played out more in thoughts and in their head. They regret the opportunities missed; they envy those who can afford it, who openly exalt themselves through their high standard of living.

Discontentment is always related to externalities, to what is loud, to the world, to "happiness" in a material sense, and to be admired by other people. Older people often have not learned to apply the divine rule of life, which we now know, to themselves, in order to develop the true values bit by bit, namely, the inner values, in themselves.

In view of this dead-end in which many an older person finds himself, what would be good advice for the youth?

Despite a life turned toward fulfillment from without, if the Golden Rule of life is not forgotten, the person will in time have the desire to often turn within, to the stillness. But he will also suddenly feel that freedom, self-possession and inner security have more value than the urge to pursue the many material desires, which in the end, keep bringing so much disappointment.

One could wish a young person to go through the following experience:

Every now and then, I can seek out a so-called quiet chamber, a quiet corner, in order to hold a dialogue with God – let's put the word "prayer" aside for the moment. God knows about all things, but I can tell Him everything because He is our kind and loving Father. I can say everything to Him and can also tell Him about my faults, my sins, and ask Him to help me so that I become more free, so that what I did yesterday, I will no longer do. That what I did the day before yesterday, for example, with my boyfriend or girlfriend for my own sake, that is, out of my own egotistical urges, I no longer want to demand from him or her, and much more. Jesus, the Christ, says that through this, very gradually another desire will grow that brings us closer to the inner life.

Every now and then the young person could – if he wanted – withdraw into the quiet little chamber and take a look, for example, at his usual day's routine. He may see how he simply sat down at the breakfast table early in the morning and then took off; how he got through what he needed to do that day and how he tried to influence things so that everything would turn out as he wanted it. Perhaps suddenly, from the very basis of his soul, the thought could rise in him to begin the day with the Spirit of truth. He then withdraws a little and speaks to God.

"Lord," the young person may say, "if You do exist, then I want to begin the day with You. But don't be so strict with me. You know me; I am still young and want to fulfill this or that desire.

There's only one thing I'd really like: Remind me of the Golden Rule of life, give me a slight 'nudge,' so to speak, when I cross the line. I will try to pay attention so I can catch it!"

Misunderstandings can happen among people. But God never misunderstands us. He knows what we mean when we say something to Him. He knows how to take it. He sees into our hearts. And He is full of kindness, mildness and forbearance.

God, Christ never takes what we do or say badly; He never scolds us; instead, He comes toward us as a good friend. He knows us so well, as a person could never get to know us. If we have felt this, that is to say, experienced it, then we feel we are in good hands with God despite our imperfections. We could also say that we know we are secure in Him.

Christ can give us very earnest, admonishing impulses, but only if we are willing to accept them. He knows the right moment. And, if we are open to it, He will also warn us, because He wants to keep us from harm and guilt, like a good friend. He knows how to guide His human children who want to be guided by Him. According to our state of consciousness or our momentary state of awareness, we will then receive His help, His advice, including His admonishments or warnings – through the events of the day, through seeming "coincidences," or through sensations and thoughts.

To go through the day, to go into the evening and night with Christ brings a good, higher awareness of life and the certainty that we are never alone.

All of this applies to the young, to older people or even to the elderly. But the young person whose emotions and conscience, whose subconscious, yes, whose soul, is not so burdened by wasted opportunities or guilt from this life on earth, has it much easier to find his way into an uninhibited and free communication with Christ, a connection and heartfelt relationship that is alive and deep.

Every person is free and always decides freely for himself. Whoever recognizes the chance that is given remains free to act on it.

And what can we advise the older person who still feels driven to fulfill this or that?

We can only advise him to go to work and clear up those things that make him so restless – and this is always the past. There is some event from the past that we will be reminded of today. And whatever is shown to us on this day is what we can also go to work on and clear up the same day. If we do not immediately know how, then we can go into prayer and talk to God, to Christ. We can ask Christ to help us, so that we can see our part in the situations that we encounter on this day or that we are reminded of.

Jesus, the Christ, in this short path that is rich in substance, revealed to us the following:

The day brings many hints to every person, often of a very painful kind. But every hint – be it an ever-so-great turning point in the day or even in your whole life – has a message or answer for the one concerned.

If the emotions of the one concerned come into turmoil, then he cannot fathom right away what message this situation or that difficulty wants to convey. Later, when he has calmed down, perhaps in the even-

ing, what the day reflected to him may then become apparent.

Jesus, the Christ, continued:

To close the day becomes a necessity for the one who applies active faith and the rule of life, so that he may correctly sort through in his consciousness the disagreeable situations, but also what was agreeable. Through this, he can become calm again, which for every person is the key to the inner stillness that the Christ of God is in the very basis of each soul – the I Am, the Spirit, which speaks to the people through the prophetic word and is giving instructions in this text for a higher life.

Christ spoke of the inner stillness and of a higher life. Why the inner stillness?

Many a one who practices becoming still and who strives toward being still says: For me, this means, that I can be reached by God or Christ only in the inner stillness – not by hearing His word in me – but perhaps by becoming aware in my thoughts of situations that I can work on, or that solutions to problems come to me. I can perceive all this only in the inner stillness, because if I am constantly occupied with externalities in my thoughts, in terms of what still needs to be done and taken care of or attained, then Christ cannot help me. He cannot show me where the next step is that I need to take in order to draw closer to this higher life.

And so, we could say that the key to finding our way into the inner stillness is the dialogue with God, also in prayer. Particularly in the morning, the dialogue with God, prayer, is very significant, because He, the Spirit, should lead us during the day. And if He can lead us during the day, we can sense what the higher life means. Our senses become refined; our character changes toward the good; we become more sensitive, and we more often apply the Golden Rule of life: *Do not do to others what you do not want to have done to you.*

This gradual refinement and ennoblement of the person is his pathway toward spiritual ethics and morals. The spiritual ethics and morals, the refined character of a person, also includes the unity that encompasses nature and animals. For in spiritual ethics and morals, also lies the refinement of the senses that shows us, for example, that we should not kill the animals and eat their carcass.

Isn't it an absolute mockery to partake in church of the host, in which allegedly is found the body of Christ, and then go home, open the refrigerator and take out a carcass piece of a fellow creature to eat? The Holy See has no objection to this; church leaders do the same. But that is the institutional doctrine of the church, and has nothing to do with the active faith that Jesus, the Christ, taught us.

At this point, many stop short to ask: "Does this really happen? After partaking of the host in church, do people really go home and take meat or sausage from the refrigerator to prepare a carcass meal?"

That is totally normal! Everyone knows about Sunday roasts. And where does this come from? It corresponds exactly to the tradition that is so far from the consciousness of unity. Some young people even experienced it in Cologne during the summer of 2005 on the "World Youth Day." In the home of an Archbishop, the "Holy Father" found a refrigerator stocked full with all the best sausage and meat specialties of the region.

What a difference between this posture toward our fellow creatures and that which Jesus, the Christ, taught us!

Actually, every person – and above all, the youth – seeks out ideals and role models. What better ideal or role model for the youth, but also for older people, than Jesus, the Christ?

And in contrast, what idols are put on a pedestal by the institutional churches? A so-called "Holy Father," who after finishing an idolatrous worship service, goes home and eats his fellow creatures. This is what marks the idol – as opposed to the spiritual ideal.

And what did Jesus, the Christ, say to this?: *On your life's path to God, our eternal Father, you should know that no person can take away the "for and against" of another person. Nor can a pastor or priest take away from you what you have voluntarily inflicted upon yourself, for they are likewise sinners, and, as sinners, can forgive only those who have sinned against them.*

And Jesus, the Christ, continued with His revelation:

A human being is absolutely free to do or not do, as he prefers. From the mighty Creator, the human being received a conscience and a mind as a scale for weighing his thinking and doing. In addition, he also received the guidelines for weighing and measuring, the commandments of God and the divine wisdoms of life that I, the Christ of God, taught and still teach. These point out that the human being is himself responsible for what he does or does not do.

This responsibility for oneself is something that perhaps not all people want to take on. This is why they leave it up to the pastor or priest, or perhaps even the "Holy Father" to think and act for them. But Jesus, the Christ, explained to us:

… Nor can a pastor or priest take away from you what you have voluntarily inflicted upon yourself, for they are likewise sinners, and, as sinners, can forgive only those who have sinned against them.

The day shows us what we should do. This is why it is so important for us to question ourselves over and over again: "Do I make use of the day? I am responsible for everything that I do or do not do each day. And if I am responsible, then no human being is of any use to me, even if he calls himself a pastor or a priest or even the 'Holy Father.' The only thing that is of any use to me is the Spirit of God, the Christ of God, in the so-called small, quiet chamber, who wants to go with me, who is with me during the day. He helps me, through the Golden Rule of life, to do what makes me free, happy and glad, what truly lets me live."

Christ revealed:

What does trust mean?

Trust has to do with trusting. Do you trust Me, that I can do everything that serves the well-being of your soul? You will now sit up and take notice, for you have read "for the well-being of your soul." Don't protest, perhaps by already raising an accusation in the question that asks, for example: "And the human being? Is the human being, the physical body, worth nothing?"

Let Me explain to you: The soul has an eternal life. As it purifies itself, it becomes a spirit being again, which is the absolute image of the eternal Father. The more the soul purifies itself of the transgressions against the law of love and of life, the more it becomes filled with light, which means it becomes brighter. This means that ever more light of eternity radiates into it. It is the light of the Christ of God, which I Am, the Spirit in the very basis of your soul. If the soul can be imbued more and more by the radiation of the light of eternity, then the light also radiates increasingly into the body, into the cells of the body and into all the components of the human body. The light of your soul is positive, divine energy, which then also fills your body with light and power. Now you can understand, when I say "for the well-being of your soul."

If a person retains his faith and trust, and if he lives more and more according to the commandments of God and My teachings, then the statement "for the well-being of the soul" also includes the body, the person. Then it means: "for the well-being of the soul and of the body," because now the light also increasingly radiates into the body, into the person.

And so, trust is a link to faith. Without active faith, which, as mentioned, means going through a "lean period," trust cannot grow.

I want to give you another help to develop faith and trust on your path to God, your eternal Father. It is: Hope and endure.

The path "have faith, trust, hope and endure" is the direct path to the love for God and neighbor. However, the rule of life is always in first place: Do not do to others what you do not want to have done to you.

What is hope?

A part of hope is setting goals, which means that you have not yet reached your goal. There can still be *smaller or larger hindrances on your life's path, which will come to you only at a later time. However, know that every day lived spiritually is a step into the security that is God. The one who wastes his days is uncertain and thinks: "What can come to me today or tomorrow, anyway?" When you walk the path to life, you will live more consciously, step by step, thus gaining the certainty that God is with you. The path within to God in you will always give you ever more strength to question your thoughts, words and actions, in order to clear up those aspects in them that make you all too human. The one who takes on this task each day changes his character to the positive.*

Hope contains confidence. Confidence can also be called forbearance, the hope that God, when the time has come – when the time is ripe, so to speak – will direct everything toward the good.

A person's intellect is not capable of fathoming what can still come toward him, the person, during the course of his life on earth, that is, what the future will bring. This uncertainty is a state of expectation. For many, uncertainty borders on the unbearable. If a person is not strengthened in his faith and trust, then he grasps the nearest solution to eliminate as quickly as possible what is moving him, what has hit him in his spirit or physically. In this moment of decision – whereby the fear, the uncertainty, is the dominant force – he is convinced that what he has in view is the best thing for him.

However, the one who has attained strength in God knows that hope, or hoping, means to test oneself. The turning points in a person's life on earth show him whether he is merely pretending to be on the path to a higher life and to what extent he is fortified in his faith, trust and hope, or how quickly he seeks a worldly solution, because it is taking too long until God is able to direct him. This kind of weighing and measuring often results in the death of hope on the untilled field of human conceptions.

Sooner or later, many a one will recognize that this path he chose, the solution he sought, brought only a brief fulfillment of hope and that he has received from his untilled field of all-too-human, sinful concepts. Symbolically spoken, this means that it was stones instead of bread. The one caught in this network of viewpoints that are far from God frequently has a hard time turning back to faith and trust, because over the mistake of the unfulfilled solution lies his disappointment, *which is often so great that trust in God can be reestablished only with the utmost effort.*

People who turn away from the path to God in disappointment – because they hope from God, the Eternal One, that He should do and solve things the way they see it and would like to have it – escape back into their everyday life. They are satisfied with the traditional, through which hope in the helping Spirit often dies. At some point, their everyday life brings to light the abnormalities of their human nature. People who do not rely on God become anxious, grouchy, embittered and querulous. This all-too-human, discordant daily behavior speeds up the aging process; it leads to depression, misery, illness and perhaps even a premature death.

A person in the maelstrom of a thinking that is turned away from God seldom realizes that the Spirit of the Christ of God, who I Am, knows every person from the very bottom of his soul and thus, also knows beforehand how this person will act during the course of his path through life, above all, when the time comes to test himself.

If a person has gone hand in hand with Me a part of the way to the eternal Spirit in the very basis of his soul, then his whole behavior, his character, including his five senses, have changed toward the positive. Many a person who experiences this thinks he has attained a breakthrough to the light and to perfection. So that he is not subject to self-deception and does not neglect his efforts to grow closer to God, the Eternal, his personal goal-inputs keep making him recognize and experience where he stands, and that situations and events often take a different course than what he expected.

Know that the Spirit of infinity knows what is good for you.

Oh see, I want to guide you, because with trust in Me you should master the hindrances that may still lie before you. No master has yet fallen from heaven, but the Master from the heavens, the All-wise and All-knowing Spirit, wants to make you spiritually strong, so that you are able to endure the hurdles resulting from your having turned away from God – the unlawfulness, that which is still lying as hindrances on the path to the higher life – enduring them with inner certainty, active faith, steadfast trust and strong hope.

Original Christians talked about the words of the Lord in the small roundtable discussion. Here is what they said:

Christ, our divine brother and Redeemer, spoke about the well-being of the soul. Some of us, above all probably the youth, were more or less shocked when they heard: ... *for the well-being of your soul.*

The revealing Spirit, the Christ of God, explained to us why it is *for the well-being of your soul.* What He brought near to us was and is very important. Let us bring to mind what He said:

If a person retains his faith and trust, and if he lives more and more according to the commandments of God and My teachings, then the statement "for the well-being of your soul" also includes the body, the person. Then it means: "for the well-being of the soul and of the body," because the light now also increasingly radiates into the body, into the person.

And so, trust is a link to faith. Without active faith, which, as mentioned, means going through a "lean period," trust cannot grow.

Many people rely on their body and ask Christ that He heal the body. If the body attains no healing, many a one even comes to doubt in the power of the Christ of God. But let us realize that the mighty Spirit thinks first of the soul, which is the bearer of eternal life, of the freedom, the beauty, the purity, the inner nobility, as seen in its totality, of the divine heritage.

If the soul is burdened, the healing power cannot, or can just barely, flow into the body, so that the healing power can hardly become effective in the body. And so we are called on to not only look to our body, but to become aware of what lies on our soul. For the shadows on the soul allow the healing light to shine into the body only very weakly.

On earth it is also so, that wherever the sun cannot shine there is mustiness and hardly any growth. So trusting in the Christ of God, who is the inner physician and healer, is of great significance. And in this trust grows the realization of what I have done in my life that was wrong, of where I have violated the law of eternal life, that is, of what shadow lies on my soul.

Whoever seeks and asks, will find, because the eternal Spirit wants to help every human being to recognize the shadows of his soul and to remove, to dissolve, them with His light, to transform them, so to speak, so that the eternal light can flow more and more into the body, bringing soothing and healing.

And so, every person is asked each day how he wants to use his day. The person who abandons himself to the day, by striving to more or less get the day over and done with, does not live in the day. He does not live consciously. He continues to sin with the content of his feelings, thoughts, words and actions, and through this, produces one shadow after the other, that only burden the soul more and more. The person who is alert and uses the day to recognize what the day is showing him is a wise man. Step by step, he builds his house upon the rock, upon the Christ of God, by asking for help and support, and by no longer committing the errors that he did until then. Through this, the shadows dissolve and the helping and healing power can shine into the body in order to also lead the person to the higher source of life. For every human being is only a guest on the earth, and life on earth passes away. The lasting gain is solely the eternal, the divine life.

At some point in time, each person will have to follow the path to a higher life. This begins with faith, trust, hope and endure. With regard to this, Jesus, the Christ, taught the following in His word of revelation:

The path "have faith, trust, hope and endure" is the direct path to the love for God and neighbor. However, the rule of life is always in first place: Do not do to others what you do not want to have done to you.

Thus, the rule of life is a general lawful principle of divine life. It encompasses the whole cosmos. We begin very simply with a question addressed to ourselves:

How do I behave toward my fellowman? How do I behave toward the world of animals and plants?

Whoever watches himself, his world of feelings and thoughts, his whole way of behaving, in order to learn, realizes that there can be no separation, no differences made. I cannot say: "I am good and kind to my fellowman," but I exclude the nature and animals worlds and cause them suffering and harm in some way or other. Because then, in myself, I am being untruthful. If we people want to change something on this earth, to find the direct path to the love for God and neighbor, then we can do this only by including the "environment," that is, all life forms, in this life. This includes the animals, the plants – all of nature. All these life forms are constantly there for us. They serve us.

Particularly in this area, a crass wrongdoing of human beings becomes obvious.

Often we hear the statement: "I don't do anything to harm an animal or plant. I am an animal friend. I love not only my housepet but all animals, too. I can't bear to see any little animal suffering."

To this, a question for the young people, as well as for our fellowmen in middle age and old age:

Who likes to eat meat? In other words: Who likes to eat animal carcasses?

Many a one may vehemently resist bringing his love for animals into connection with eating meat. Why? The majority of people are not aware, for example, of where the piece of meat on his plate comes from and that an animal had to suffer unspeakably and die a torturous death for this. For this reason, let us just very briefly look into what happens to the animals whose meat is consumed by meat-eaters.

Take, for example, animal farming. Hundreds of cows are kept in one large barn, packed together. They stand on metal gratings over a huge manure pit, into which their excreta fall. It stinks accordingly and flies and other pests are everywhere.

The so-called feed concentrate that is given to them as food would not be eaten by the cows if they had a choice. To cut costs, they receive the cheapest waste-products, which are barely edible, to supply the body with the necessary nutrients for producing milk or being fattened for slaughter.

The cows, artificially inseminated year after year, bring their babies into the world in this place. Let us feel into a small calf that has just been born – a small animal that, like us humans, is born to see the light of the world. This small living being is immediately taken from its mother.

Before it is slaughtered, the little one is kept isolated in a wooden box in a dark barn, and is fed an artificial food instead of its mother's milk, because the consumer, the animal cannibal, demands white, tender veal. The young animal cannot move. It is kept in the darkness, apathetic and without drive, because the normally trained muscles of a calf that runs around the meadow would cause tough meat. Moreover, the calf is kept anemic through a strictly iron-free diet and by using a wooden box without any pieces of metal because the young animal, in its need, would lick any piece of metal it came into contact with, to get the necessary trace element of iron into its system.

A worker at a factory farm said that when the newborn calf is taken from the mother, both mother and calf cry for three whole days. The mother cries for its baby and the baby for its mother. And what did the animal farmer then say?: "Well, it's not very nice to listen to their cries. But after three days it is quiet again."

Perhaps as a reader or listener you are now feeling indignant, but another statement from an "animal ghetto warden" literally was: "We don't have to treat the animals well. After all, they are here only to eat, drink and die a wretched death."

When reports on the great disaster in New Orleans went through the media in 2005, a reporter commented the following: "We have to say the people here are dying a wretched death." When this is about human beings, we are horrified. Is it supposed to be normal with animals?

The Golden Rule is: *Do not do to others what you do not want to have done to you.*

Let's talk about this divine rule of life again. We could ask the following question to the mothers and fathers who simply eat the meat of their fellow creatures without thinking: What would you say if this were to happen to your children? The rule of life is very short and succinct and without room for exceptions: *Do not do to others what you do not want to have done to you.*

How great would be the suffering of a mother whose child is taken from her? As human beings, each of us should every now and then become aware of the fact that animals feel very much as we humans, as human mothers, as human fathers, and as human children. The animal mother, the cow, for example, or a mother pig, wants only to do everything possible so that her children feel well. But in the factory farms, every possibility for this is taken from them.

The meat that is mostly eaten in Germany is pork. Sows are also kept in very narrow sties called "birthing sties." The mother cannot even touch her piglets, her children, because she is squeezed in so much that aside from nursing the piglets, practically no contact is possible. The reason given for such narrow confinement is that the mother doesn't crush the little ones – which, of course, is more likely to happen under such narrow confinement. Under normal conditions, every mother would very tenderly care for her newborn young.

This is also seen by observing wild pigs that live out in the wild. The children have a "home" where they feel safe and well, where they can romp about, watched over and cared for by their mother, the wild sow.

But what happens all to often instead? Hunters come and shoot down the sow or her young.

This is true for all animals, for deer, rabbits, foxes, etc. The animals of the woods and fields are hunted, shot down or "merely" mortally wounded, until they finally die in torment. Their meat is then eaten by the human beings.

To all people, who know about these cruel murders and condone them through their silence, Jesus, the Christ, said in His rule of life: *Do not do to others what you do not want to have done to you.*

Up to this point, we have referred to the animals in the factory farms, on the fields and in the woods. But we should not forget the animals that have no voice – it is those in the waters. Fish suffocate torturously when they are taken out of water. Sometimes, their gills are slit open so that they slowly bleed to death. Since the fish cannot scream and cry out, as opposed to mammals, they do not receive even an anesthetic when they are killed. What a crass contradiction to the golden rule of life of Jesus of Nazareth!

And no one can say: "I wash my hands in innocence because I personally don't do anything to the animals." We need to be aware of the fact that every person who eats meat is giving the order to kill; we actually should say to murder, because the animals are defenseless and unsuspecting. If we kill a defenseless victim, we can call it murder.

Murder in the waters and on the land. Is there murder in the fields as well? What happens on the fields, in the soil, when they are covered with chemicals, with liquid and solid manure? The smallest of living beings, our animal brothers and sisters – very much our fellow creatures! – are suffocated, burned, killed in the cruelest ways, using the cruelest means.

Chemical salts in high concentrations, that are supposed to promote the growth of plants, harm and kill the micro-organisms in the soil. Through pesticides that are supposed to destroy the so-called pests, micro-organisms also perish wretchedly.

Even large animals have a hard time out in the wild. If, for example, because of the interference of human beings in the natural balance of nature, a certain animal species suddenly becomes over-populated, like mice or wild pigs – they are exterminated like pests and cruelly slaughtered, either by using poison or bullets. Human beings, who constantly maltreat nature and bring it out of balance, then claim that they have to proceed against nature and animals with their deadly weapons for the sake of bringing nature back into balance.

Today, an enlightened person knows all this, and yet he encourages it, if he accepts or buys the products connected to this, that are marketed by those who violate nature for their own profit.

The same is true of the torture that animals suffer in laboratories, in homes, in the barns, everywhere. Whoever tortures animals creates causes – and at some point in time, this torture will start up against this person.

Why? – What a person sows, he will reap. What a person has caused will subsequently come back to him as an effect or a blow of fate. Often, he simply closes his eyes to this and does not want to admit it is true.

Jesus passed on the words, *Do not do to others what you do not want to have done to you,* also as the following: *Do to others as you would have them do to you.*

What is it that a person would not want to have done to him by others?

No person wants to be done in, to then be eaten. But no person wants to be tortured either, or to live under such unworthy conditions as people force on the animals. A person doesn't want any of this. Neither would a person be prepared to make himself available as a guinea pig and undergo torturous procedures. Nobody wants any of this.

He doesn't want it himself, but he does it to others. What happens then? The law of cause and effect is set into motion. People don't want to hear about this, even though many are Catholic and rely on the so-called Saint Paul, who even said it clearly to the people. In the letter to the Galatians we can read: *Do not be deceived. God will not be mocked. What you sow, you will reap.*

And so, we could say that worldwide the seed is germinating more and more. And once it does, we will experience the real character of many.

Many people have no goals. They simply live through their day and do not understand what the day wants to tell them. Each day, they behave in a way that is more and more against life and do not think about what Paul said to the church and Bible believers: *Do not be deceived. God will not be mocked. What you sow, you will reap.* These words of Paul, which the churches deliberately ignore, speak the truth, and this truth applies to all people.

If people were to use the day by asking themselves what it is that their day today wants to tell them, then they would come to understand that life on earth will one day come to an end. Then what?

A person who will strive to set up goals during his young years will also pay attention to the sentence: *Do not do to others what you do not want to have done to you.* Or, according to the words of Jesus: *Do to others as you would have them do to you.*

Jesus, the Christ, spoke in His revelation to us human beings:

Every day lived spiritually is a step into the security that is God. The one who wastes his days is uncertain and thinks: "What can come to me today or tomorrow, anyway?" When you walk the path to life, you will live more consciously, step by step, thus gaining the certainty that God is with you.

The path within to God in you will always give you ever more strength to question your thoughts, words and actions, in order to clear up those aspects in them that make you all too human. The one who takes on this task each day changes his character to the positive.

During our time, a person can experience how important it is that we change our character to the positive. Particularly in situations of need, the true character of a person becomes evident. One would think that in an emergency situation every person would be there for the other and each person would help the other so that everyone could survive. But with the great hurricane disaster of 2005 in New Orleans, for example, what many people experienced was that this did not happen. Instead, the true character of the people came through, which in many instances contained only "me, me, me," the ego, for which the survival of the individual alone was important, even to the point of not excluding the death of another.

In addition to this, Jesus the Christ revealed the following:

The turning points in a person's life on earth show him whether he is merely pretending to be on the path to a higher life and to what extent he is fortified in his faith, trust and hope, or how quickly he seeks a worldly solution, because it is taking too long until God is able to direct him. This kind of weighing and measuring often results in the death of hope on the untilled field of human conceptions.

The occurrences in New Orleans in particular are such a testing ground for the weighing and measuring just referred to. Although the people in that area swear so much by the Bible and although it is well known that many groups of Bible-believers exist there – did they take the path toward a higher life? Or did they rely on sham human values – perhaps even including what Bible-bound priests or pastors had explained and may have lived for them as an example?

Remember the statement of Jesus, the Christ: *You will recognize them by their fruits.* So what we can say is that the fruits we saw there are more than shaking, because most of what we heard was about illness, need, plundering, rape, violence, quarreling and fighting among each other. The people in need did not grow together; they did not help each other; instead, each tried to save his own skin. In this exceptional situation, where the character of a person should have shown higher, nobler features, it was often the opposite; the all-too-human aspects came to the fore only too clearly.

So again we are faced with the questions: Are we at all aware of the fact that we are merely guests on this earth? Have we recognized the objective of eternal life – or do we still rely on the all too human, the ego, which we have perhaps expanded upon throughout our whole life?

Many a one could say that in old age, the ego dies out. But whoever talks with people about their life realizes that many older people become more and more infirm. With increasing infirmity, their ego comes to the fore, which gets very nasty, very self-righteous toward others, embittered; it is a very biting ego.

This is in accord with what Christ said in His revelation: *People who do not rely on God become*

anxious, grouchy, embittered and querulous. And He
went a step further: *This all-too-human, discordant
daily behavior speeds up the aging process; it leads to
depression, misery, illness and perhaps even to a
premature death.*

So many a one who has a lot of spiritual knowledge tries to suppress the negative symptoms and
acts in a particularly kind and friendly way – but
only until he is directly addressed about his weak-
nesses; then often, this saintly, external conduct
makes a complete turnabout into anger and
wrathfulness.

The alternative to our all-too-human, earth-
oriented life, which the Christ of God points out
to us over and over again, is the eternal life. This
is a goal worthy of our striving during our life
on earth; it is our true being.

What is eternal life?

Young people have the urge to live. Life for
young people means at first to live on a material
level. Young people have many desires that are
part of their life, and that is quite all right. It is

the striving forward of a young person. However, not only a young person, but every person could ask himself, particularly when he is doing something against his conscience: "Is this right? Should I act toward my fellowman, toward the animals, toward nature, just as I feel at the moment?"

These questions alone show that a person's conscience is still active. Here, the Golden Rule of life could be applied. This does not mean that a person has to totally abstain from the pleasures of life on earth, or that he has to give up the desires that a life on earth brings with it. But he should consider: "What will this bring me in the future? Difficulties? Problems? And of what use to me are the problems? Do they weaken or strengthen me?"

The Golden Rule is the perfect help for making decisions. "And how do I feel when I decide for the good, the right thing? Don't I feel light and free?" Keeping the Golden Rule of life can very well lead us to pass by difficulties and problems, to pass by many a trouble.

It is especially the young people who ask: "What's with eternal life?" A question to young people would be: Do young people have no fear?

Experience has shown that the youth aren't as afraid of life after this life as many an older person is. Young people have rather the hope that something wonderful is waiting for them. The fear that this may not be attained normally comes in later years, when one begins to notice that this or that which should have been done, wasn't done.

In our youth there is hope for an eternal life, a part of which is activity and not merely singing "Halleluiah" on a cloud, like many know from the movies. A young person imagines that life in the eternal Being is filled with activity, dynamism and productivity, that there are inconceivable possibilities there, which are not available on earth. And they're not that far off base either. The scope of possibilities increases just through the fact that one does not live under the limitations of space and time. A life in the divine brings with it a whole new dimension that, among other things, contains the unity of life.

One imagines eternal life to be something incredibly wonderful. But in order to draw closer to this, each one has to do something toward it already during his life on earth.

Eternal life is, indeed, a great thing! As soon as the soul is again the spirit being, that is, divine, it joins in the great, mighty mechanism of heaven, in the mighty creation event of the eternal Father, whose Spirit is constantly breathing in and out. New suns and worlds are unceasingly created in the spheres of heaven. Whatever is recently added to it is cared for by the divine beings – this is what their activity consists of, among other things.

The development, the evolution, of a divine being takes place on the planes of development – from the smallest component of a spiritual atom to the perfectly developed nature being that grows into the divine principle of duality, into the divine being, which fits into a principle of mentality.

In the homeland, in the eternal Being, in infinity, there are large divine families. They work in the eternal, divine kingdom according to the mentality of each of the family members.

Every spirit being is integrated in the All-cosmos and is heir to infinity, which says that the essence of life, which is cosmic, is the make-up, the structure, of a divine being.

The eternal homeland, the Being, is the goal of every soul. All of the Inner Path, given by Christ again in its short form and expounded upon here in the small roundtable discussion, wants to give us the chance to return there, to where we all once came from. To keep this goal alive in us may be easier for us if we know that the kingdom of light of the heavens, our eternal homeland, is waiting for us in the innermost recesses of our soul. Every alert soul longs unendingly to be back home again.

This is why it is so wrong and presumptuous to strive toward prestige, power and wealth. Because all of this passes away. And in the end, what is the person? An impoverished soul. On the other hand, how rich is the soul that orients itself to the eternal life that is beauty, purity, fineness of character, nobility of mind and all-encompassing love.

Endure

First, a passage from the Christ revelation of August 2005 again. The Christ of God spoke the following:

What does it mean to endure?

To endure means to bear one's own fate without demands and accusations toward one's neighbor. To endure also means to help bear with sincere mercy the suffering and fate of others. Many a one may ask: Why doesn't God take away my fate – or that of others – from one day to the next? Why must the encumbrance or the physical burden, often with pain, be borne for a long time or even for an entire lifetime on earth?

Recognize that you are not on the path for yourself alone. Many people are walking the path to God in the innermost part of their soul. Many a fellow traveler needs a person's help. If you bear your fate, your burden, through your faith and trust in Me, the Christ of God, the Spirit of love in you, and if you persevere with confidence in God, until the time has come when the Christ of God stands by you according to the law of love and of life, just as it is good for your soul, then you are fortified with trust in God. From this, your spiritual treasure chest of experience, you can also help your companion on the path, your neighbor, if he wants it. This is genuine guiding help.

You heard correctly: if your neighbor wants this. Freedom is a part of the law of all-encompassing love. A spiritually experienced companion on the path has become spiritually sensitive. His feelings and his five senses are part of the ennobled qualities of his character, which I also want to call the fine antennae. The refined character – distinguished by justice, freedom, helpfulness and serving love – is the unfolded spiritual consciousness, which has become capable of perceiving and can thus fathom many things, for instance, in the various situations and everyday problems, in himself and in his neighbor.

The unfolded spiritual consciousness is also capable of fathoming whether the person seeking help wants to accept it or not. If a person approaches a spiritually awakened person from within as well as externally, and if the latter notices in his neighbor's patterns of speaking and acting that he is seeking support and help, then fine and trained senses are needed to sense the extent to which the person seeking help is willing to accept the advice and help of his partner in conversation.

On the path within, to God in you, you will become more sensitive level by level. On each level of development – for example, that of active faith, of trust, hope and endure – you will learn to recognize yourself more and more, and later, to experience and understand your neighbor in you. Particularly by enduring, that is, by persevering and relying on God in what hit you, lies wisdom and experience, but also the evidence of the love for God, your Father and Mine, the Father of all men and beings, and also of the love for neighbor.

The soul in a human being is on the earth to become a spiritually mature fruit. If, following the death of the physical body, the Christ of God is able to pick the ripe fruit, then the soul no longer casts the shadow of death over the sinful body which is gradually decomposing. The soul, which bears the light of the heavens, goes heavenward at My hand. People who have kept the rule for life day after day – Do not do to others what you do not want to have done to you – are filled with grace. As a human being, they have received grace, love and wisdom from God, and as a soul, they will continue to be guided by God's kindness and strength on their way to the Father-house, until they immerse in the infinite sea of love, to eternally exist as pure beings, as sons and daughters of God.

A person who in his earthly existence orients himself to the commandments of God and My teachings, primarily the Sermon on the Mount, is spiritually mature and has become capable of selfless love, which unites all people, beings, and the nature kingdoms with their plants and animals, and which encompasses the All-Creation. The love of God is unity; it is the All-creating power and the All-creating will of the Almighty.

The following is a recording of the conversation of the small roundtable discussion:

In His revelation, Christ asked the question: *What does it mean to endure?* And then He explained: *To endure means to bear one's own fate without demands and accusations toward one's neighbor.*

What do young people have to say to this sentence?

Most young people understand the term "to endure" to mean that a person goes with his hat in hand and lets anything be done to him, that is, that he has to "let himself be beaten into submission." It seems you have to endure something that someone decided for you and that is fully unjust and against which you should rebel. This is what a young person thinks about when he hears the term endure. But, of course, something completely different is behind this statement in the Christ revelation. It means to bear your own fate and overcome it, and not a fate that someone else imposes on you.

A young person could object and say: "Well I rebel against this, and rightly so. Why my own fate? My fate was imposed on me – maybe by my parents who weren't as I would have liked. And my colleagues at work, who boss me around and demand of me what I don't want to or can't do. I'm right to rebel against this. It's not my fault that I have this fate!"

Whoever argues like this is actually claiming that his life is based on pure chance. In other words, he would be saying: "Whatever I encounter in life actually doesn't have anything to do with me, and is based on some coincidental occurrence or other." But we know from the divine revelations that every person shapes and forms his own fate. What we readily accept as the law of cause and effect in physics concerning matter also holds true in the area of spiritual correlations.

This means there is no effect without a cause. Someone who has to endure an effect is also the one who caused it.

Most probably at this point, a young person would ask the question: "But when should I have created the cause?" – And this leads us to reincarnation.

The causal law and the concept of reincarnation cannot be separated from one another. The law of sowing and reaping and the reality of reincarnation are fact and not theory or speculation; instead, they are physical correlations that hold true everywhere in the Fall-realms.

We can observe every pattern of behavior in daily life and recognize over and over again that no energy is ever lost. For example, when we heat a piece of ice, a solid piece of matter, it will liquefy; it turns into water. When we heat the water, the liquid matter, it becomes steam, a kind of gas. No one would ever think to claim that the water disappeared, because we know that if we are in a closed room, for example, the moisture in the air condenses on the ceiling and at some point in time will fall down as water drops. Negative effects are also possible. If we often steam up a room, at some point in time, the walls will mildew.

We can see that every activity that takes place in daily life has an effect somewhere. Why? Because no energy is ever lost.

When we transfer this picture to our inner processing – we could say that our negativity, our thoughts of hatred, of envy, of animosity settle in our soul – the precipitate is like "mildew."

This comparison can be drawn out even more: The formation of mildew becomes apparent very gradually. We note how it begins, how the surface of the wall loses its shine bit by bit, turning darker until in the end it is black. It is very similar with the soul. When we constantly emit negative energies in feelings, thoughts, words and deeds, this negative energy, among other things, settles in our soul and in our disposition. In time, our whole character becomes rather "mildewy." But this also means that our soul grows darker, and through this, heavier.

Remember the steam: When water turns into steam, it goes into another aggregate state. It is similar with the soul: When the body dies, the soul moves into another aggregate state; but the precipitate of our sinfulness, the darkness, the "mildew," is taken along by the soul.

A soul with a lot of "mildew" thus carries a great deal of earthly weight. Matter, coarse material substance, is heavy. Matter always attracts matter. This means that the soul will at some point in time again be attracted by matter, for example, by a person, that is, a soul that has already incarnated again and with which the former had caused some things in a previous incarnation. It comes together with these people in order to now clear up the whole debt or a part of it.

We can more or less describe reincarnation this way. From these correlations, it becomes clear that we bring our fate with us, and whom we meet or with whom we may have difficulties is not by chance. The difficulties a person inflicts on us or the weight we have to bear with someone are those which <u>we</u> may have very well burdened the other with in previous incarnations.

And so, let us learn to endure in the spirit of the teachings of Christ! Let us learn to more or less accept our own fate by asking: What was it that I caused? What is it that I have to recognize, repent of and clear up? Without this conscious work on ourselves, we will be able to leave the cycle of reincarnation only with great difficulty. For this reason, the Golden Rule of life, *Do to others as you would have them do to you,* is significant. It is a great help. It consistently refers us back to ourselves. It stimulates us toward self-recognition and we then immediately know what it is that we now have to do or not do.

In His revelation, the Spirit of the Christ of God went some steps further. He not only showed us our life's path, not only how we can dissolve our own fate – namely by clearing up the dark sides – but beyond that, He said: *To endure also means to help bear with sincere mercy the suffering and fate of others.*

According to Christ, another aspect of endure is: *To be considerate of the other, by letting a statement or conduct continue without opposition.*

This is, of course, difficult to do. We can very well explain, but not hit back. To endure also means to take no counter measures, to merely explain, so that in time, the other recognizes that he also is partly to blame himself.

And so, when we endure something, this doesn't mean to do nothing and simply stick our head in the sand. Instead, we can explain the situation from our own point of view, but not hit back. The result is that the person who has learned to endure can use the scales to weigh and measure: "How far can I go with my explanation? Where is my own self-interest behind this? Where do I begin to hit back? What can my neighbor understand and accept, and where do I hit him? What do I possibly use to blame him for something?"

We should always quickly question ourselves before we react or call the attention of the other to his faults. For as it is written, *take the beam out of your own eye first.*

Christ continued speaking:

To endure suffering without making another responsible for it. To rely on God quietly and meekly in illness and suffering, which says, in turn, that faith and trust are necessary for this. Or: To bear quietly, devotedly and steadfastly, in the hope that God knows a way.

To not endure would mean that I do not allow something, that I rebel against something, not accepting it, and so on. For example; "I will not endure my neighbor stealing from me – I will attack, hit back, defend myself." Much of this is right, but at the same time, we should question ourselves: "Can it be that I may have taken some things from my neighbor in a previous incarnation? Did I, for example, keep something important from him and used it for myself so that I would be well off?" This does not mean that we should deliberately let someone steal from us. We should pay attention and take preventive measures, but not apply violence.

Remember the behavior of Jesus of Nazareth: As Jesus stood before the high priest, He was beaten. He endured these beatings but He also explained. He asked the one who had beaten him: *Why are you beating Me? If I committed a wrong, then tell me.** This is a good example of the fact

---

* *"If I have spoken wrongly, bear witness to the wrong; but if I have spoken rightly, why do you strike me?"* (John 18:23)

that one cannot simply accept everything, but should also not hit back in such a situation.

The unteachable one will, of course, ask the following questions: "Why doesn't God take away my fate or that of another person from one day to the next? Why does the encumbrance or physical burden have to be borne for so long, or even a whole life long and often with such pain?"

This indicates that our whole life is about learning: learning to live according to the spiritual fundamental rules. It is from this that grows the belief in Christ, the Spirit of love in us, as well as the trust in Him.

Of course, it is difficult – particularly for young people – to bow before such a fate without rebelling against it. What advice can we give a young person who has to bear a burden of pain, suffering or other kinds of indispositions, or even physical handicaps?

Without the knowledge of reincarnation, it may be truly difficult for such a young person to bear his fate. But knowing about reincarnation, even a young person can understand that this suffering did not come to him without reason and that in this suffering, in turn, is the task to learn.

It isn't a matter of its having to remain the same forever. There is also the prospect that once the lesson has been learned, it can get better. Particularly from such an experience, hope and confidence can grow in the young person, that much in life can change for the better by coming to one's senses and changing one's ways.

From the knowledge of reincarnation, a young person can conclude that there is no punishing God who inflicts bad things on him. This alone is quite a gain, because then he can build a winning relationship with God, which, in turn, helps him bear many a thing in life, and learn many a thing, as well. If today, an improvement of circumstances has perhaps not yet been given for this life, he can work toward a better start-up for his next life, for the time his soul is in the soul realms and for his continuing path to the eternal homeland.

And let us not forget that a great help for each person is the fact that the Spirit of God in Christ, who is also our Redeemer, is the Inner Physician and Healer, the inner helper, who wants to support us in every need and in all affliction.

If this fact becomes more and more familiar to a young person – and to an older person as well – then he also becomes increasingly aware that he is not alone and that he does not have to carry his burden alone. He knows about the power of the Christ of God in himself that wants to help and support him. He knows that it is not Christ or God who has burdened him with this sorrow or suffering, but that instead, He always wants to help him to become healthy and happy – and in the final analysis, to become again a being in God. The eternal Father wishes most profoundly that His daughter, His son will soon be very close to Him.

How can we draw closer to the Inner Helper, the Inner Physician and Healer, Christ, or how can we draw closer to God in us?

Again, it is important to keep the Golden Rule of life: *Do to others as you would have them do to you.* Or said differently: *Do not do to others what you do not want to have done to you.* And of course, this includes everything that we find in the Sermon on the Mount of Jesus of Nazareth and in the Ten Commandments of God. If a person follows these divine commandments, he draws closer to Christ in himself. What he then experiences gives him the trust that Christ is there, that Christ helps.

We can also help a young person, if he wants it, by encouraging him, for example: "Just try! Pray more often! Pray for yourself; pray for your fellowman – even if he doesn't mean so well by you – or, perhaps, particularly because of this. Pray for the animals that you love; pray for all of nature. Simply try it; in time, you will feel better. And above all, pray as you feel it in your heart. Do not use any pre-formulated prayers, but speak to God or Christ as you would to a good friend, to whom you can say everything."

Seen in this light, to endure has absolutely nothing to do with this blind, dull, passive submission to fate, which results from a mere faith that tends to say: "Everything is coincidence" or "That's just a part of the mysteries of God." And so, to endure in the spirit of the Christ of God implies activity, which means: "I take my own fate in hand and change it for the better by turning to God."

If I know that I do not have to bear everything alone, this takes away a lot of the heaviness and bitterness from the situations that make it difficult for people. After all, I have someone who helps me: the Spirit in me. This does not mean, for example, that a young person now affects piety, that he shows himself before other young people as being devoted to God or as a totally different person, so that the others point their finger at him. Spontaneity in a young person should be kept up; but he should learn to weigh things.

The result of this deliberation is a treasury of spiritual experiences, as the Lord referred to in His revelation. If we have learned some things from ourselves, if we have learned to endure our own fate and to transform ourselves with His help, then we can also help our neighbor, if he wants us to.

If there is something about him we disapprove of, we will not hit out at him right away, or yell at him, or do something that harms our neighbor. We will briefly take ourselves back and say to ourselves: "This does not correspond to my character. This does not correspond to the rule of life." Otherwise, a young person can do a lot of things during his years of "sowing wild oats," as it were. But what would always be important is the question of whether he causes harm to another.

We very briefly touched upon the fact that a person who has learned to endure can help his neighbor from his treasury of experience, if the latter wants this help. Christ expressly indicates in His revelation: *You heard correctly: if your neighbor wants this.* What does He want to tell us with this sentence?

He wants to make us aware that to endure also means we should not force ourselves on another, in order to make him say or do something that he may not at all want to.

For many of us, this is an important sentence, because often, when we see that our neighbor is having a difficulty or problem, we react from our own correspondences. Something is stimulated in us that perhaps is just as sinful. We then think that we have to share our "wisdom" with our neighbor, which perhaps isn't really even carried by true recognition and knowledge, much less already overcome in ourselves.

Why should we not force ourselves on our neighbor? Because the law of God is freedom.

Christ continues in His revelation:

Freedom is a part of the law of all-encompassing love. A spiritually experienced companion on the path has become spiritually sensitive. His feelings and his five senses are part of the ennobled qualities of his character, which I also want to call the fine antennae. The refined character – distinguished by justice, freedom, helpfulness and serving love – is the unfolded spiritual consciousness, which has become capable of perceiving and can thus fathom many things, for instance, in the various situations and everyday problems, in himself and in his neighbor"

So, this means that only with the fine, ethereal senses is the deep perception of another possible; everything else is assumption and does not build on an inner understanding, on an inner sensing, and on an inner recognition of one's neighbor. In this inner perception, also lies the certainty of how I can help my neighbor, what I can say to him, what internal and external help he needs.

Many a one may now very well ask: "How do I get to the fine, ethereal senses that, in time, shape my character and make the inner perception possible?"

Here, too, the application of the Golden Rule of life is decisive: that those things I don't want to have done to me, I don't do to my neighbor – and vice-versa: To come to understand more and more what it is my neighbor needs, in order to be able to then give it to him, so that it is a real help.

We can start with our senses: I see something that I don't like and then I think accordingly: I disparage my neighbor or I negatively judge what I see. How would it be if we were to say to ourselves: "Well, it's about time to start questioning myself. Why does my neighbor concern me? I cannot point out to him that what he is doing is wrong, even if I perceive it as wrong." Provided I get upset about it, I can ask myself what lies behind this. And if I then clear it up, and again perceive something similar, I will no longer condemn it to the extent I did before.

Consider our sense of hearing: I hear this or that. And what happens? We start thinking about it, and usually a value-judgment quickly follows. Why do we do this?

It is because we do not think about ourselves, because we always tend to judge our neighbor and do not see our own part. Actually, it is because we do not apply the Golden Rule. The Golden Rule would always mean to ask myself: "How would I feel if another were to judge me in the same way?"

A young person could say, for example: "I don't care!" He can, of course, say this, but it should be clear to him that by doing so, he is harming himself – and that he will not attain a true and deep perception either, but will only judge and condemn via his external senses.

A refinement of the senses also means that you should question what you see or hear that upsets you, and clear up your part, because every agitation indicates a correspondence. What upsets me about the other person is what corresponds to <u>my</u> nature, to <u>my</u> character. If I change this, then my character changes for the positive. The same is true for smelling, tasting and touching. Whoever refines the first three senses – of sight, hearing and smell – in time, will no longer eat meat. He will dissociate himself from the enjoyment of "meat" – and why? Because it no longer fits with his character, which has changed in a positive way.

If we do not strive toward this development of our character, then what happens to us? We will grow ever more dull. We can see this everywhere: The human being is becoming ever more coarse, ever more brutal. It is not by chance that brutality and violence today are gaining the upper hand in the world. This means that these negative characteristics are triggering each other more and more. They grow into huge clouds and are not only intensified in the individual but also in his close surroundings and in whole nations. In the end, we are then driven and controlled by negative, by brutal and violent energies.

Since our five senses are the antennae to without, our whole structure becomes coarser, more negligent; we judge and condemn and disparage others, until it turns into hostility and war, murder and manslaughter.

Our development is totally different when we apply the divine rule of life, as well as the commandments and teachings of Jesus, the Christ.

Then, our senses become refined and very grad- ually turn within. This means that they turn to the core of life, the primordial stream of the soul, the Spirit of God in us.

Once the bridge has been built, from the fine, ethereal senses to the divine in us, we attain deep perception. We no longer judge or condemn. We see more deeply. We perceive, for example, the person as a whole, his negative sides, but also his positive ones. We then know how we should behave toward the other. The fine, ethereal senses also split open problems, situations, work proce- dures, and take from this the essence that leads to more: into another work procedure, into anoth- er good conversation – as a whole, into a good course of life on earth.

And so, this means: *On the path within, to God in you, you will become more sensitive level by level.*

What does "more sensitive" mean?

There is a difference whether a person is sensi- tive to what is around him or hypersensitive about certain issues. Hypersensitivity becomes evident in the overreactions of a person to every- thing that comes his way, by being particularly concerned or sad and letting it come out to the extent that his fellowman notices it. Being sensitive to what is around us brings a deep, conscious and clear perception.

Via the ethereal senses, via the bridge to the primordial stream, to the Spirit, the sensitivity, the perception, develops. Do I have this spiritual perception, this depth, this farsightedness, that is, the insight into situations, occurrences, into procedures at work, into people, and so on? And how do I then express myself toward my fellow-man?

In the concrete situations of the day, I remember the rule of life and relate it to myself: "What I don't want others to do to me, I won't do to any other." This means that we will not simply blurt out something, hitting our neighbor over the head with what we don't want to have said to us or to hear from someone such harshness or ruthlessness. So how would we express ourselves?

We would be more sensitive, reserved, understanding. We do not hit someone over the head with what we say, because with this, we cut off his freedom. Through sensitivity, we are given the words that can be a key for our neighbor, so that he must not obstruct the way to us and we find our way to him. This then leads not to being against one another, but to a sense of connection where communication is maintained.

And so, through sensitivity, through deep perception, we attain the spiritually cultured language. We will no longer express ourselves in vulgar terms, but will describe the matter or illuminate it from a spiritual point of view.

The spiritually cultured language is the language of the Spirit through us in our perception. And so, if the bridge to the primordial stream, to the Spirit in us, has been built, then the help, the support flows over this bridge, and not lastly, the impulses of the Spirit, so that we can, for example, approach a person in such a way, that we leave him his absolute freedom.

The eternal Spirit does not express itself in a vulgar way. It has no clichés, no strong words. It simply has another language content, and we acquire this via the ethereal senses, which are also linked to our brain cells.

The spiritually cultured language has nothing to do with the manner of speaking that many describe as an "educated language," which, however, his neighbor doesn't understand, because it consists of foreign words and expert terms, which the speaker may have studied, but which express nothing to his neighbor.

So, the spiritually cultured language is not an expression of intellectual thinking, but the language of spiritual intelligence.

The intellectually cultured language shows off – the spiritually cultured language helps. The intellectual language excludes its neighbor and is an artificial language that can be understood only among an elite sworn to it. And it is exactly among this "elite" that the one does not understand the other. Each speaks only himself, and no one really knows what the other wants to tell him.

If you should not know what we are referring to, then consider the highest form of intellectual absurdity: the dogmas and teachings of the Catholic Church. No one understands them because – and this is also typical of an intellectual education – nothing is really behind it.

The spiritually cultured language, on the other hand, can be experienced in the divine revelations. Christ told us how we can develop this perception in His great revelation:

On each level of development – for example, that of active faith, of trust, hope and endurance – you will learn to recognize yourself more and more, and later, to experience and understand your neighbor in you. Particularly by enduring, that is, by persevering and relying on God in what hit you, lies wisdom and experience, but also the evidence of the love for God, your Father and Mine, the Father of all men and beings, and also of the love for neighbor.

For us, this means that we strive to constantly question ourselves and apply the rule of life so that we attain the sincerity, honesty and truthfulness that are based on freedom.

Every person dies. What are the *shadows of death over the sinful body which is gradually decomposing?*

Isn't it the bad conscience that always knocks, because we feel that over the course of our life we have done and thought many things that were against the Golden Rule of life? What develops from this bad conscience is fear, above all as a person grows older, because death keeps drawing nearer and because the conscience is pressing ever more. That is why, in the end, we want to keep our body.

And so, fear is the shadow that clings to the sinful body for which the hour has come to pass away, so that the soul may gradually attain recognition in the purification planes or enter a new sinful body again, a body that decomposes. This depends on what the soul bears, how much "mildew," or weight, burdens the soul, which at some point in time will again be attracted by matter.

For this reason, we can say that the more fear a person has for his body, the more he can be sure that he will soon incarnate in a new body, because he clings so much to matter and to the earthly life.

The law is: "like always attracts like," and so matter always attracts matter. So it can be said that the more burdened a soul is, the more earthbound it is, and the more it tends toward the earth.

On the other hand, how different is the prophecy of the Christ of God in His revelation to us, referring to those souls that are imbued by the stream of life:

The soul, which bears the light of the heavens, goes heavenward at My hand. People who have kept the rule for life day after day – Do not do to others what you do not want to have done to you – are filled with grace. As a human being, they have received grace, love and wisdom from God, and as a soul, they will continue to be guided by God's kindness and strength on their way to the Father-house, until they immerse in the infinite sea of love, to eternally exist as pure beings, as sons and daughters of God.

What do we understand by the words *the infinite sea of love*?

The infinite sea of love is the spiritual homeland, the law of love, where all beings live in this law and where no malice and no evil exist at all; where spirit beings live in perfect unity with animals and with nature, and where God is present in all their hearts.

And so this is the cosmic All-law that is immutable, that every soul has to achieve someday, because in the very basis of the soul pulsates the law of unending love, that the Christ of God describes as the infinite sea of love.

The following books can be ordered directly:
www.Universal-Spirit.cc.
1-800-846-2691

Universal Life
The Inner Religion
P.O. Box 3549
Woodbridge, CT 06525

Universal Life
P.O. Box 5643
97006 Würzburg
Germany

Books by Gabriele, the prophetess of God

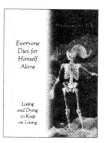

The Contemporary DEATH
Everyone Dies for Himself Alone
Living and Dying to Keep on Living

The contents of this book are relevant for every person who wants to get away from the fear of death and grow into a conscious life, into a sense of security, a peace of mind and inner steadfastness. For: "Whoever learns to understand his life, need no longer fear death." The reader of this book will find explanations and insight into the until now unknown correlations between life and death, into the condition and health of the soul under the many different circumstances surrounding the process of dying and about what awaits the soul in the beyond once the physical body passes away.

160 p., Order No. S 368 en, ISBN: 978-1-890841-48-5

Cause and Development of All Illness
What a person sows, he will reap

What philosophers and scientists have tried unsuccessfully to figure out over millenia is revealed in this book, directly from the divine-spiritual world: The emergence of the material universe, the correlations between spirit and matter, the interchange between soul and body, and so on. Beyond this, a fullness of previously unknown details is given about the frontier regions between spirit and matter, about the development and emergence of human beings, about the course of events set in motion by human beings through their interaction with their fellow man and with the forces of nature, about the power of thought in the life of the individual and his surroundings, about details that are given on the past, present and future of the earth and much, much more. An exciting and fascinating reading!

Cause and Development of All Illness

340 p., Order No. S 117 en, ISBN 978-890841-37-9˜

The Gospel of Jesus
The Christ-Revelation
which the world does not know

This Is My Word
A and Ω

The Gospel of Jesus

The Christ Revelation,
which true Christians the world over
have come to know

A book that lets you really get to know about Jesus, the Christ, about the truth of his activity and life as Jesus of Nazareth. From the contents: The falsification of the teachings of Jesus of Nazareth during the past 2000 years - Pharisees, yesterday and today - Jesus loved the animals and always supported them - The meaning and purpose of life on earth - God does not punish or castigate. The law of cause and effect - The teaching of "eternal damnation" is a mockery of God - Life after the death of the body - Equality between men and women - The coming times ...

1078 p., Order No. S 007 en, ISBN: 978-890841-38-6

The All-Spirit, GOD, Speaks Directly Into Our Time Through His Prophetess

He does not speak the word of the Bible

The All-Spirit, GOD,
Speaks Directly Into Our Time
Through His Prophetess

He does not speak the word of the Bible

14 divine revelations given from 1987 to 1997 have been put together in this volume. What is remarkable about this collections of revelations is their often full relevance to the explosive events of today's time. For example, about current events on the world's stage, about the intolerable conditions on the earth, the abuse of the teachings of Jesus, the Christ, by the institutional churches and much, much more. As no other, this book conveys the nearness of God and His deep love for each one of His children. An exciting read for truth-seekers regardless of religion, race or nationality.

256 p., Order No. S 137 en, ISBN: 978-1-890841-36-2

The Inner Path
Collective Volume

On the Inner Path, life becomes interesting: A total of 24 Original Christian meditations serve to prepare the soul and align it to the true, inner life. This is then followed by the basic levels: Through precise exercises and explanations, you learn to get to know yourself – thus, finding your way step by step to a fulfilled life, to true peace and long-lasting happiness, and the unity with your fellow man and with nature.

Seven books in one volume: * Two Original Christian courses of meditation * Basic Level Of Order * Basic Level of Will * Basic Level of Wisdom * Basic Level of Earnestness * The Great Cosmic Teachings of Jesus of Nazareth to His Apostles and Disciples, Who Could Understand them.

1344 p.. Order No. S 150 en, ISBN: 978-1-890841-07-0

Alone in Marriage and Partnership?
Alone in Old Age?
Living in Unity!

Alone in Marriage and Partnership! Alone in Old Age? Living in Unity!

Generally speaking, our life on earth consists of a chain of disappointments for us people. We have hopes and longings and yet, we are always dissatisfied. We desire something – mostly from our fellow man – like happiness, love and security. For a while, we think we have finally "found" it, but then, our expectations are not fulfilled and we are alone again. So why does

You are not alone – GOD is with you

this happen? The roots of our longings lie more deeply than what can be given by the world. Everyone who wants to, can follow the deep wisdom of this book and discover for him or herself how to find the way into the unity that is God and that brings happiness, peace and contentment.

164 p., Order No. S 367 en, ISBN: 978-1-890841-47-8

Books by Gabriele, the prophetess of God

Pirouettes of Life.
My fate, your fate, our fate. Whose life plan?

The Old-Timer and the Prophet

Animals Lament - The Prophet Denounces!

The Murder of Animals Is the Death of Humans

God's Word, the Law of Love and Unity,
and Those of the Earth Without Rights

The Love for God and Neighbor
and a Bent, Distorted Christianity